HAIRY MONEY

The Handbook Every Stylist Needs
to Stay on the Cutting Edge

by David Bronson Maestas

HAIRY MONEY
The Handbook Every Stylist Need to Stay on the Cutting Edge
by David Bronson Maestas

Copyright © 2018
Medio Inc. LLC

ISBN-13: 978-1512380231

Printed in the United States of America

Table of Contents

Dyeing to Know Your "Why"

Everyone has a "why" - what is *yours* ?" Why are you doing hair?

Can you think back to the days of beauty school and remember what motivated you to start cutting, coloring, and perming hair?

I hated beauty school. It was basically an extension of high school with blow dryers and brushes. But just like the rest of you, I made it through that miserable experience.

I think my "why" is similar to many other people's and perhaps your own. College was not for me. I was all signed up to attend Colorado University and was starting in the fall of '98 when I decided in August of that same year, right before I was supposed to start school, that I would check out Americana Beauty Academy. The next thing I know I'm standing in the middle of a 1970's style classroom in an ugly black smock with about 30 other 20 something year olds and a bag full of brushes, combs, and who knows what else.

I asked myself, "What the hell did I just do!?"

I had a moment of regret. The beauty school counselor was very convincing and before I knew it she had me signing a contract which officially stated that I was a registered student of Americana Beauty Academy in Colorado Springs, CO. Thus started my career in the salon industry and the many paths that it would lead me down.

I was raised by parents who also did hair so I had some idea what I was getting into…but 18 years later as I am writing this book and in reality I had no idea what I was *truly* getting myself into. My parents were really disappointed that I was becoming a stylist because they kept telling me that I needed to use by brain and not my body to make money.

I wanted to work in an industry that was fun, creative, and familiar. I wanted to be around other people who were inspired and loved their work. The hair industry seemed to fulfill all those things for me.

When I was 19 I came "out" to my family and my mom was really worried that I was going to have a hard time making it in the world. Being gay is not exactly the easiest path in a society where it's not the most accepted path. I was scared of being ridiculed and rejected and I didn't want to have to hide who I was at work.

Being a stylist has given me the opportunity to not only express my sexuality, but in this industry I was actually valued for my expertise and sexual preference. Who knew I could actually go to work and feel safe, loved, and accepted for being gay. The beauty industry is a safe haven for many gay men and for that I feel it has given me a great gift and I want to return the favor by giving back to other stylists what I've learned not only as a stylist but as a coach and business owner.

I've done it all in the beauty biz. I've done Miss America pageants, worked for Christian Dior doing seasonal runway release work, acted as Technical Advisor for Schwarzkopf, done hair for a reality series on MTV, weddings, celebs, photo shoots, and even talk shows. I apprenticed with a well-known celebrity stylist and also trained other stylists as well. I've been an owner, commission stylist, and worked booth rent. I've traveled to do hair and stood behind a chair all day. I've made nothing and made hundreds of thousands in a year. I've had my own product line and had friends who've made millions with their own line of beauty products. I've been around the block and I have to say, it's been quite the adventure.

I've written this book so that you can learn some of what I've done to be successful and maybe even learn from some of my mistakes. I want to help stylists grow and make lots of money whether behind the chair, on the set, or on TV.

You have a valuable place in the world. You impact lives whether you know it or not. Your opinion matters. Sometimes you are the only confidant your client has. You come into contact with CEOs, moms, attorneys, doctors, real estate agents, flight attendants, accountants, and almost any line of work that exists. You have the world at your fingertips, literally.

Now I want to show you how you can leverage this power so you can be a success and live the life you've always dreamed of. I have personally worked with stylists that have increased their income by 300%, and their product sales by 400%, in as little as 6 months. Can you imagine the trips you could take, the car you would buy, or the money you could save for retirement?

Hopefully, along with making people feel beautiful, making enough money to live a comfortable life should be one of your "whys." Isn't that why we all wake up and go to work in the first place? The potential to have a successful and fulfilling career as a stylist is highly possible. Everyone needs a haircut and people all over the world have hair. From kings to contractors, we all get haircuts. The world needs your skill!

You can take your talents and scissors with you anywhere in the world. It's a benefit to being skilled as a stylist and you can make money anywhere you have your scissors and a comb.

So why are so many stylists out there having a hard time making enough money to make ends meet? Why are there so many stylists that struggle to pay their bills? That is where I come in. I have watched the hair industry change and evolve for almost two decades and I've found common themes and a formula for success that will work for you. It works with all professionals not just stylists. These tools can help you become the kind of stylist who takes control of their destiny.

Are you ready to find that kind of success for yourself? If you are reading this book then I am guessing you are. You are ready for real results and you are ready to live a more financially abundant life. There is nothing wrong with wanting to get paid what you are worth and I will show you how you can finally have the kind of breakthroughs you have been waiting for.

If you are ready and the tools are here to help you then this is the perfect marriage. You are the student and the teacher has appeared. I believe that nothing in life is an accident. Everything has a divine timing and that time is now. There is a reason that you are reading this book. Something is pulling you forward for more and you are ready!

I applaud you on taking the first steps toward making your life the kind of life you want to live. If you do what you love, you will love what you do. Stylists live a fast-paced and creative life. We work with our bodies and our minds in a creative capacity. We listen to people all day and they learn to trust our skills and our advice.

The reason I ask what your why is, is because I want you to create a vision statement for your business. This will be the foundation for your successful career. This foundation will be a reminder why you decided to become a stylist in the first place. It may be for the fun, it may be for the money, or it may be to make people feel good. Whatever your why is, that is the reason that will drive you to continue doing what your doing.

When you start getting discouraged, tired, and things seem to be getting tough or when your clientele is wavering and there are gaps in your day this vision will be your guiding light. It will be your beacon back to the reason you are standing on your feet for 8+ hours a day and the reason you receive the reward of watching someone transform before your eyes.

Take a moment right now to travel back in time to the days before you even started beauty school and see if you can find the reason you walked through the doors of that beauty college. Was there a relative that inspired you? What is the reason you decided to get into the beauty industry?

After you have found that special reason, write it down here or write it in a notebook and meditate on that statement. Make it at least one or two strong statements that sum up the whole of your career in hairstyling and why it drives you. Your vision statement might sound something like:

> I love my career as a hairstylist because I find the work inspiring, creative, and fulfilling. Every client is a new canvas that I get to create on and I feel a sense of gratification from completing a beautiful service. I make a handsome income in a safe environment and I find joy in

my work!

List your why here...

_____
_____
_____
_____
_____
_____
_____
_____.

The reason I am asking you to find your why and create a foundation statement for your career is because it gives you purpose. Without purpose many people start to deteriorate and find no reason for living or trying anymore. Not having a purpose can be the cause of depression and other mental ailments. With a vision statement you can start to see why you are still cutting and coloring hair. You are the creator of your life.

The words and actions that you meditate on begin to create your conversations and your actions. Then your actions start to become your habits and they in turn start creating the life you are living. If you have no idea why you are doing hair in the first place then why would you continue doing something that has no purpose?

Think of it this way - when you get into your car and you start driving, you usually have a destination in mind and a reason why you are taking the trip. Could you imagine a bunch of cars just driving around with no purpose or direction? Oftentimes that is how we live our lives, and that is why so many people cannot get the success that they are desiring. They don't see the bigger picture.

If you get off course on your journey, just take a few turns here and there and you're back on track towards your destination. Think of this thought: if you have no vision for why you are driving what is the point? Your vision is the reason you are driving. Money may be your why. Maybe your kids are your why. It doesn't matter the purpose, just make sure you have one.

I will touch more on the subject of your journey later on in the book when I talk about setting and accomplishing believable goals. For now, let's get your vision clear and renew your purpose. You will start feeling the energy returning to your body and you will start feeling rejuvenated and recharged.

If there is a part of you that starts to feel emotion wash over you when you make your vision statement, it's the part of you that is being healed and it is reminding that part of you why you are here. When you realize you have value you start to feel a sense of gratitude for everything in your life including your career. If you've been doing hair for more than 15 years like I have, sometimes we forget what it's all for and we lose focus.

That emotion you are feeling is waking up the inspired energy that you forgot was there when you start dealing with the everyday monotony of the salon. We forget we love what we do when that old hag is back for her fifth redo this month and she is costing you more money than she is worth. We forget we love what we do when that new shade of red was way too cool and now she wants a color correction. We forget we love what we do when that jerk working next to us will not sweep up his hair and refuses to clean his color bowls.

Everyday stuff can build up and cause us to lose focus but now that you have your vision down in writing you can remember the bigger reason why you are here. Why you are reading this book. Why you are a stylist.

Now that we have a vision, and I've brought up the subject of the everyday grind of doing hair, that leads me right into my next chapter: Salon LIFE.

Dyeing to Live the Salon L.I.F.E.

Salon life can be a bitch, I'm not gonna lie.

I think we have some of the hardest yet most rewarding jobs in the world. We literally create masterpieces all day long while holding a decent conversation, staying on a cramped schedule, and using our creative and scientific minds for eight or more hours day after day. We stand on our feet without taking a lunch or sitting down for a break - sometimes all day!

Kudos to us for being some of the most kick ass people in the work field and doing it with impeccable style and unfathomable grace.

You make changing the world look easy. Think about the impact you have on the world as a whole. You actually create the way people look. When people look at pictures of themselves they see your work. When someone goes on a date and falls in love with the way the person sitting across from them looks they fell in love with some of your work. When you watch TV, go to a movie, or open a magazine, there is your work again. You create beauty in the world everyday!

That's a pretty steep responsibility and one that shouldn't be taken lightly.

That sets me up for the first letter in the acronym **LIFE**, the "L".

The "L" stand for LOVE.

If you are not absolutely in love with what you do everyday when you stand behind the chair then it's time to look deep within and see if it's time for a career change. Not just because you are probably miserable but because when you love what you do, it feels effortless. You will find it rewarding.

I know a lot of people who ended up in beauty school and didn't even know why they were there. They ended up being some of the most talented and amazing stylists I've ever known. I've also know people who wanted to be a stylist from the time they were old enough to pick up a brush and they are the most lousy stylists I've ever seen.

So why do I say that you should love it? Because even though I've seen people who couldn't style their way out of a box of bobby pins, they have a clientele that would humble the Queen of England. They draw clients like bees to honey.

What is their secret?

I will tell you…they knew they loved hair from the time they could remember and that love is like an intoxicating fragrance to anyone that comes into contact with them. People can feel the love all over them and they want to be near that. People love to be around other people who are inspired and living their highest purpose.

People who love their career in hair also exude confidence even if their work looks like a can of silly string on their clients head. It's all about the flow - and they are in it!

Now, let's go back to the stylist who is amazing at what they do but don't even have a purpose for being there. Yes, they may look like they are successful but doing hair is draining the life out of them. It may be their clients who drain them. They may be physically tired or they may struggle to keep their books full. Whatever the drain in their business is, it's there, I guarantee it.

I know people who make lots of money but they are so drained by the work that they have to get drunk and party most of the time they are not at the salon because they are not fulfilling their highest purpose. They have to "numb" out just to face another day.

If you've ever worked with one of these stylists, they are usually egotistical and complain about every client. They drain everyone around them and they resent 90% of the people that sit in their chair. They are unbalanced and think that the world owes them. They treat their clients like they're lucky that they even got an appointment with them. These are the symptoms of an unbalanced stylist with no love or gratitude for what they do.

Let's go back to the stylist who loves what they do and they find value in their service to the world. They are the example of what it is like to find your life's passion. I like to call it our "divine purpose." We are all created to fulfill a place in the world and these inspiring stylists have that "thing" that other stylists don't have.

These wonderful magicians of hair don't find the challenges discouraging. They find them as opportunities to grow and find new creative ways of doing hair. They find an opportunity to grow in every haircut and color service.

If you watch someone who is in the flow, they seem to be

lighter than air and the work energizes them. Would you like to become one of these inspired beings of hair utopia? YOU CAN!

Even if you are not necessarily loving the industry you can definitely learn to love what you do. If you are not ready to jump ship just yet, you've worked long and hard for a solid clientele but you are not feeling inspired anymore, there is hope for you too!

I get so excited about this concept because it all comes down to what your highest priorities in life are.

Let me rewind a little bit...

I know so much about being one of those stylists who resent the world and every hair in it because I used to be one. I get it!

It took everything I had in me to drag my hungover butt out of bed every morning to miserably drive to work and put on a happy face so I could make just enough money to pay the bills and go to the liquor store about 4 times a week. This was my sad life.

I was a young, talented, and brilliant stylist but I was also miserable and drunk most nights trying to forget about the stressful day and all of my needy clients.

I was basically just surviving. I had lost my vision. How many of you reading this book feel like you are just surviving right now - trying to pay the bills and stay afloat? Been there done that. I remember one month I spent more on liquor than I did on my mortgage! Talk about drowning out the sorrow...I was the king of it.

I would justify it all by saying that if I worked hard, I could play hard. I know in the hair biz we definitely don't have a problem finding time to party and cut loose. As a matter of fact we're kinda know for being a party crowd. We are addicted to living on a high and we applaud ourselves on being fun and entertaining but without balance we can start to feel drained and worn down.

If you are one of the stylists who is feeling worn out, beat down, and uninspired, please pay close attention to the next part of the this section...

It's time to find what we really *do* love. If doing hair is just a job, then what is your *true* love? If you have kids, is it raising your kids? If it's finding love, then is it dating? Is it travel? Do you like spending time shopping or eating out?

Here is a list of things that might resonate with you:

- Working out
- Shopping
- Travel
- Raising kids
- Building a business
- Spending time with friends
- Happy hour
- Eating at new restaurants
- Gardening
- Video games
- Meditation or prayer
- Spirituality
- Decorating
- Cooking
- Movies
- Theatre

- Luxury vehicles
- Sports
- Golf
- Skiing
- Tennis
- Fishing
- Hiking
- Biking
- Yoga

This list can be endless...

What is it that really makes your butter melt? What is that thing you could do all day?

When I started to ask myself this same question about 5 years ago, I started to realize that I love to teach. I love the concept of helping people discover themselves and to look deep within to see what makes them tick. Sometimes this is easy and sometimes it's hard. But I just love to teach!

So now that you have identified those things that really make you feel purpose and passion in your life, let's find out how your job, doing hair, can benefit your highest priorities.

If I say that my highest priority is going to the gym and being fit then how can I tie what I do for my vocation to what I love most?

It's very simple. I tie the two things together and I see how one gives me the freedom to do the other. It may look like this:

"I love working at a job that keeps me active, helps me

burn calories, and gives me the income I need to join that amazing new health club in my area."

Another example might be parenting. If parenting is your highest priority then you might say:

"My job gives me the flexibility and freedom to pick my kids up after school. I learn new parenting ideas from my clients and I have an income that allows me to save for my kid's college fund."

If your passion is travel, it may sound like:

"I love talking with clients about their recent travels and it inspires me to plan my next trip. I also love that I make plenty of money to travel the world."

Can you see how these two things work synergistically together, hand in hand? Take a moment right now and think about what your first love is and write it here.

_____.

Thinking about how your job is serving your highest priority is the key to falling back in love with what you do. It will start to weaken any resentment or boredom you feel. When you can find the benefit in what you do and how it is giving you the freedom to do what you really love, you will see the beauty in making people beautiful.

This re-focus of energy also helps to grow your business. When your thoughts are directed to what is most important to you, you will find ways of making it grow. It becomes valuable and you will care for and nurture it. You will be more apt to try harder if you can see that your career is feeding the most important aspects of your life and not just helping you pay the bills.

Focusing your energy works something like this...

Do you remember when you bought a new car and after you bought it you started seeing that car everywhere? That is because that particular car is now part of your awareness. Another example is, did you ever think about cutting bangs and you started noticing all the different kinds of bangs on girls everywhere? That's how focusing your energy works. Your mind starts to see what it wants to see and it starts to show up everywhere!

So if you can find the benefits of your job then you will start seeing more and more benefits from your job. You will start acting in a way that says, "My job benefits me and makes my life what I want it to be." You start to see opportunities. You start talking about it differently and clients will be drawn to your energy. People will start to see that you value your job and that you value them. They will be more committed when they feel that you're more committed.

If you love what you do then you will find success in it - it's that plain and simple.

When you find benefit in your work then the hard stuff will just roll off your back and you will glide right through the day like a kite on a sunny day. When you focus on what is rewarding then even the struggles seem worth it and I will tell you why...

Have you ever had a really bad headache, one that just wipes you out,and the pain is so bad you can barely stand it? Well imagine if you had one of those headaches and all of a sudden you found out you won the lottery! How much do you think you would be focused on the pain of your headache? Not at all. The pain wouldn't even matter anymore.

When you're focused on what gives you reward and pleasure in your job then those bitchy clients, that lazy receptionist, and the inconsistent product rep are no big deal anymore. They are in the background of your mind and all you are thinking about are those benefits and how your job is helping you to do what you love the most.

Doing what you love most makes you feel good, and that brings me to the next part of the acronym, the "I".

The "I" stands for INTEGRITY.

The way I see integrity in the hair industry is all about fair trade. Are you charging for what your work is truly worth? If you want to feel good about what you are charging then you have to see that the work is worth your prices.

If you are doing a partial highlight where you throw 3 tired foils in the mohawk section, one foil on each side of the head, and then charge 150 dollars for it, I probably wouldn't come back to you. It's not putting forth the effort that is worth paying 150 dollars for. Some stylists try to justify it by saying that they are busy or double-booked but if you are not offering quality to your clients, they will start to notice.

The reverse happens when you don't charge what your work is worth. The bad thing about not charging what you are worth is you will start to feel yourself being thrown off balance. You will feel a drain of energy because money is the balance of energy being put forth.

When you are getting a lot of money for hardly any work, your emotions will start to tell you that it isn't fair trade and you will start feeling guilt.

This is business 101, fair and marketable trade. As stylists we tend to go for the fun and creativity of our jobs and skip the business stuff. After all we went to beauty, not business school, right?

Offering a fair price in your market and your expertise level is vital for attracting new clients and for building a repeat client base that will earn you the money that will fuel your passions in life.

Remember, as stylists we are not selling a tangible product that you can take home and walk the dog with, we are selling our knowledge and our blood, sweat, and tears. We are offering a service and the only way to price a service is to give what is paid for in your current market.

Charging what you are worth not only works in fairness to the client but it works in your favor too. If you say that a partial highlight is 150 dollars and you give them a discount for their service because you only had to use one color or you just highlighted their hair four weeks ago and they don't have that much regrowth then you just cheated yourself!

Just like the negative emotions started to tell you that something was off balance when you overcharged for your services, you will start to resent your clients and your job if you do not charge what you are worth when you give discounts or undercharge.

Living in integrity is about being fair and also being respectful of other people's time.

Oftentimes in the salon there are circumstances that fly way out of our control and we run behind. It's not the end of the world. You have to realize that the next client waiting has a life too. They deserve either an explanation, or if it is merited, I will offer a cash discount either for their service or a credit towards their next visit.

Being respectful to your clients' time and money will also ensure that they respect you and your business. You are not there to play hairstylist and give your services away for free because you have so much fun doing hair (which is what our clients think because we are good actors and actresses). You are there to make an income and live a fulfilling life and money is a big part of that.

Being on time for your first appointment of the day is also important for the integrity of your business. How would you feel if you showed up for surgery and your doctor came flying in the back door running five minutes late with a hangover, alcohol on his breath, and threw together a few implements so he could rush through your surgery and get to his next patient.

It's the same thing with hair! You can't expect to do good work when you are rushing and playing catch up all day long. Are you booking enough time for your services? Are you needing to charge more so you can have longer appointment times? This kind of sloppy behavior will take its tole on you and your business.

One of the things that I believe created the most success for me is going in about 15 minutes early on days that I have clients scheduled. I walk in cool, calm, and collected and I set my station up, have a glass of water, use the bathroom if I need to, and get everything cleaned up and ready to go so when my client comes in I'm ready for business!

This simple and practical ritual is the pinnacle of my work day and it allows me to mentally see my day the way I want it to go. You are the dog wagging the tail and not the other way around.

If you come in flustered and rushed with no makeup on and your hair is a mess then what does that say to your clients who are there to have you make them look beautiful?

I see stylists doing their makeup and hair at their stations, which I think looks sloppy and lazy. You wouldn't go to the dentist and walk in seeing him flossing and brushing his teeth before you sat down for a cleaning would you? We have to take our business seriously if we want to prepare for serious money!

Integrity is also about customer service and treating your clients like queens and kings. They rule. We are so blessed to have them sitting in our chair.

Ask your clients about things that interest them and let them tell you about their life. If they want to relax and be quiet then allow them the space to do that as well. When I see a stylist mindlessly talking to their client with no mutual sharing going on, it's a sign that the stylist is nervous and that makes the client uncomfortable as well. Beware of becoming a vocal bully and taking up all of their time. That conversation might be the most cathartic thing going on in their life.

If there is a nice conversation that flows and a client asks how your day is going then you should feel free to share. This is a slippery slope though. Remember we are there to serve our clients and to listen to them. They are the one who is paying. They are not our personal sounding board.

Oftentimes I hear stylist bragging about their recent vacation or newest outfit. But guess who paid for that trip? Who paid for that new outfit? Your clients did.

When we learn to walk in gratitude for our clients and the things they make possible in our lives then they will want to support us, help us even more by referring new clients, and maybe even leave us an extra gratuity for our listening ear.

We are not the stars, they are. They shine, and we do the polishing. We are servants at the core and that is okay. Service to humanity is the highest calling. Mother Theresa was a powerful woman of service and she didn't even get paid for it - we do!

All people want to be heard and respected, and when we offer that with a good haircut, that is living in integrity.

Re-dos are not anyone's favorite thing. Whether you are a contractor or an ice sculptor, we do not like having to do something twice. The nature of this beast is that it will happen. Will you be able to handle them with integrity and some amount of grace?

We are not machines, we do not have photographic memories, and we do not always hit the target on the mark every single time. Not even Sassoon was that good. SO, now that we have that out of the way, let's talk about how we handle things like refunds and unsatisfied clients.

Okay, your client wants something new and different so we decide to go flaming orange with black streaks and some platinum tips, cause you know…everyone is doing it.

Then you get that dreaded phone call.

"Thank you for calling the Blah Blah Blah Salon, can we help you?"

"Yes, I just had my hair done there and my boss said that if I show up to work looking like a homeless pumpkin tomorrow then I'm fired and I might actually become one. Can my stylist get me in to fix it, ASAP?"

Now, I know what you're all thinking. That chic wanted it to look like halloween shat on her head and that is exactly what I gave her!

Regardless if that is what she wanted or not you are now being asked for a solution. As responsible business people (because whether you are commission or booth rent you are a business owner), we rise to the occasion and offer to fix her color.

If you choose to charge for the re-do color or not, that's completely up to you and your salon but remember that unhappy clients tend to do a lot more complaining and talking than someone who loves their hair. That's just the sad truth about doing business with the public.

There are different statistics floating around about the exact number of people an unhappy client will tell about your work but it tends to fluctuate from about 5-30 people. Even one person hearing that you are not willing to accommodate your client is too many.

We have an obligation to ourselves and to our business to face the problem head on and help them to keep their hair looking great. Now, if their hair is not in good condition or there are other circumstances that prevent a re-do service then by all means have them come to the salon and have a conversation about what *can* be done.

I understand there are clients who are never ever going to be happy and I will talk about that more in the chapter about setting healthy boundaries but if a client needs our help, we can do our best to assist them in finding a realistic solution. We are the professionals and they trust our expertise.

Integrity is about building a business you can be proud of. There will always be challenges but how we deal with those challenges will either set us up for failure or set us apart from other stylists and other salons. We have the power to build a successful and profitable business.

If there is a need for a refund then there are two things that you need to remember. 1) If the client wants her money back, it's no longer your money. 2) Manage your money in such a way that you have not spent it already.

This courtesy is all about respect. Respect for your clients and respect for your money. If someone wants a refund then by all means give them the money and send them on their marry way - you don't want them anyway! You just paid a small price for your freedom and peace of mind.

The second thing is about respecting your money. I've seen this time and time again in the salon where a stylist is living from tip to tip. They have no reserve money and no way of offering a refund, especially if this is a booth rent situation.

Running your business with integrity is about having money in reserve for things like emergencies. You cannot run a business without managing your money. Could you imagine if a huge company like Target had no reserve for unseen events like lawsuits or changes in the stock market. They would be bankrupt in a year and that has happened to many salons and stylists around the world.

Owners over pay themselves and live a lavish lifestyle while the bank accounts run dry and no one is there to help them clean up the mess. Stylists spend all their money on clothes and partying and then when it comes time to pay the rent there isn't any money left.

I worked with a gal who ate out every meal and I am not even exaggerating. This was a horrible habit that she just started unconsciously because in the hair industry we tend to always have a pocket full of cash and often a shortage of time.

This 30-50 dollar a day habit soon turned into a truly scary addiction and eventually, major financial troubles - to the point where she didn't have enough money for her rent, car payments, or even health insurance.

Don't let this happen to you! Learn to live frugally. Put money into savings and don't let your pleasures outbalance your priorities and responsibilities. This is a recipe for disaster on an epic level.

Even though we make great money we also have to learn to respect it. With lots of money comes lots of freedoms and that brings me to the next letter in the acronym. "F". The "F" is for FREEDOM.

With lots of freedom also come lots of responsibility. Nothing in life comes without a price. There has to be balance, a yin and yang. When you make lots of money and have lots of freedom, you have to learn to balance that out with taking care of your responsibilities. In this case I am talking about your business as a stylist.

As stylists we have lots of freedoms but we can take them for granted. Just because we don't spend our days like a banker, standing around in a suit, paying close attention to every important detail, we still have to be vigilant and careful when handling our business affairs.

I have seen people in the salon biz who spend their days half hungover, barely present, and basically half ass-ing every single service. There is no sense of self-management.

I applaud the people who put their game faces on, come in fully dressed, and are ready to treat our industry like the profession that it really is. We represent our salons and our own personal business. If we come in dressed like a hooker and haven't washed our hair for 3 days then guess what people are going to think about us? You guessed it, their not going to respect us or want to support us.

Some stylists complain that they have no clients and that they're the only one at the salon who doesn't make any money. But they are always late, always running behind, and always dressed like a two-cent tramp. With all that being said, I would hope that just because we have the freedom to dress more edgy we don't take it to the extreme. And because we have the freedom of time we don't take advantage of our client's time.

If Starbucks took 5 minutes to make a cup of coffee and all the baristas were dressed like homeless hippies, would you ever go back? Would you want to drink coffee that was made by someone who had dirty hands and lousy hygiene? I wouldn't waste my time or money.

Successful companies know that there is a standard of conduct in place for a reason. We can try and deny it all we want but the bottom line is the world expects more from a professional than mediocre.

If we want a consistent return from our business we have to have respect for the freedoms that we have. Put away the daisy dukes and the crop tops and dress professionally. We don't work in a strip joint or at the beach as a lifeguard. We have a respectable skill and we want to be paid well for what we do.

Companies also expect their employees to stay up to date with the current trends and business strategies. If they don't "keep up" they fall behind and become obsolete. Are you letting this happen to you? This is the last letter in the acronym, "E". "E" is for EDUCATION.

There is an Italian restaurant here in Boulder, CO that will annually send their employees to Italy to study the latest trends in food and wine. They pride themselves on being on the cutting edge of the culinary industry. For this reason, they have become one of the most sought out and respected eateries in the Denver area.

Because the public has caught wind of the fact that they stay abreast of all the latest trends and their staff is highly educated in their extensive wine and food menu, patrons don't mind dropping the extra cash for an extravagant dining experience.

Do people seek you out as a stylist for your expertise? Are you staying on top of the latest trends? Or are your clients the ones educating you on the latest hairstyles?

Education is so important in the hair industry. We all have something to learn. If you cannot make it to classes there are so many other resources that you can learn from. There are videos, books, and online marketing tools that can help you build your education.

How many stylists do you know that use the same 3 formulas on all of their clients and do the same 3 haircuts? This is because they have become a creature of safety and safety leads to habits. Habits are what keep us stuck.

I love when stylists have a self-righteous attitude and refuse to ever attend a class. Then when I see their work I'm not surprised Because heir styles look like they came from another decade.

Education is not only good for learning new skills but it gives us confidence and our clients will sense that. If you keep up on your skills and invest into your business it will show in the amount of money you make.

Energy In = Energy Out

This is a simple law of physics and if you invest into your business by educating yourself you will start to reap all the rewards and benefits of a full bank account and happy clients. You will be sought after for your skills and people will respect your opinion.

I know stylists who would love to do platform work but they can't even remember the last time they attended a class. They have nothing to teach. If you don't fill up your tool box with new tools then when you go to work on a new style you're gonna be using the same old tools you've been using forever.

If you fill your head with wonderful new tools, formulas, and haircuts you're going to be inspired and you will exude excitement. Your clients will be the hottest looking ones on the street! People will be begging to get an appointment with you and you will start making the money that will give you the freedom to live a more fulfilled life.

Go after what you want with a "full steam ahead" attitude. You are the one who is in control of your destiny. You get to decide how you want to shape your business and if taking a few classes can get you there then go for it and take those classes. Go after what you want. Get inspired again. Find how you can achieve the highest success in your field and people will want what you have. Make your services so valuable that you make yourself stand out in front of the crowd!

Remember the acronym LIFE. These simple concepts can make or break your business and it's all about a change in perspective. This is the foundation to a successful career.

Dyeing to Grow Your Business

Growing a salon business is just like growing a plant, it takes time, but with the right food it will grow steady and sure!

I will give you some simple tools that will help you make your business visible and help you get the word out.

The first step to growing a business is to have a plan. Take some time to write out a plan of what you want your business to look and feel like.

When I started doing hair I was *so* lost. I had no idea what I wanted to specialize in. I had no idea what kind of feeling I wanted my business to have. I had no short or long term goals. I was a little lost ship at sea.

As I started to grow as a stylist, I started to realize that I was actually more in control of my business than I realized. I could actually summon the kinds of clients I wanted, how busy I wanted to be, and the amount of time I wanted to work to make a certain amount of money.

It's like hair witchcraft! It's magic and I will show you how it's possible.

First, when you start with a plan for your business I want you to think about a business that feels natural to you.

- Does it feel believable?
- Does it fit your personality?
- Does it make sense?

For example, if you're a mother of 4 children, a wife, and a Sunday-school teacher then your business plan probably won't include riding around on a tour bus styling hair with a punk band or doing concert tours and traveling the world.

You want to be as specific as possible here. There are no limits in your imagination. If you can see if for yourself and it feels realistic then you can achieve it. I've known people who started from nothing to doing celebrities' hair and making six figures. It's all possible.

Think about what kind of clients you would like to attract. Think about the kind of hair you would like to do. Do you like punk hair or classic styles? Do you want to work 8 or 12 hours a day? Do you like double booking or taking your time with one client?

This plan for your business will allow you to start setting small goals.

Take a few minutes and write down what you want your business to look and feel like.

Your plan may look and sound something like this:

> I work 8 hours, 4 days a week. I like to take my time giving my undivided attention to one client at a time. I work with high-end clients who enjoy my classic styles

and beautiful blow outs. I charge higher prices and clients love the convenience of getting in and out in under two hours. I feel relaxed at work and offer stellar customer service to my clients. I feel elegant, classy, and I offer that feeling to the clients who come in for a relaxing head massage and an enjoyable conversation. I dress with a tailored, yet expressive style that speaks about my commitment to a solid business sense and taste.

This might sound like a great plan to some and if it's not your cup of tea, it may make you wanna barf.

Another business plan might sound like this:

I love a spunky upbeat environment with fun music and a diverse clientele base. I cater to clients who want avant-garde styles with lots of bright colors and flair. I enjoy my 12 hour days with a short 3 day work week so I can enjoy going to the beach and surfing in my free time. I love the fast paced conversations and the unique style of my work attire. I love to express the more punk side of hair and cater to people who wish to express a more risqué look. My prices are set to appeal to a college aged crowd which means I like to double book so I can increase my profit margin.

Can you "feel" the difference between these two styles of business and stylist? They both play a valuable role and they both have a place. One is not better than the other - just different!

Write what you want your business to feel like here:

_____

_____

_____

_____
_____
_____
_____
_____
_____.

The next thing that will help you get your business going is business cards. Business cards are your tangible means of getting the word out there. If you are in a grocery store and start talking about the magazine in the check-out line with the lady in front of you, pull out a card and let her know you are taking new clients. You may offer her a new client discount or not but the big thing here is that you have a small elevator pitch to get the conversation going.

They call it an elevator pitch because it's short and could be recited between floors in a jiffy. Make it short, sweet, and to the point. You want to sell your services so this random person wants what you have.

You can get really creative and have fun with it too. Your personality should come through in your pitch. You want it to be easy-going and natural so you don't sound like a robot or a commercial.

Practice your pitch with the other stylists in your salon if that helps you to get into your groove. It's easier to mess up with friends so they can make fun of you, then the hard part is out of the way.

Write out your elevator pitch and have your cards printed with any important info you want to convey. I.e., are you good with color or do you love working with keratin treatments? Are you located near a convenient highway or a trendy neighborhood?

Your elevator pitch could go something like:

> Hi, I'm David. I just started at Blah Salon in LODO (lower downtown Denver). I specialize in precision haircutting and work with a new semi-permanent toner that adds serious shine to the hair. You should book an appointment with me because this month I'm adding a complimentary deep-conditioning treatment to any color service!

If I had just met you and I wanted shiny conditioned hair I'm gonna call. I know exactly what neighborhood you're located in and now that I have your card, I have your contact info as well. It's as easy as pie.

Women love to talk about hair. Anywhere I go and tell people that I'm in the beauty industry, it is an immediate conversation starter. Girls always ask the infamous question, "What would you do with my hair?" That is a great time to do your spiel and hand them a business card. You could even recommend that they come in for a free consult where they can talk about new ideas for a cut and color.

I have personally built my business from the ground up doing this. It works.

With the invention of things like Facebook, Instagram, and Pinterest now it's easy to build an online presence. You always want to watermark any pictures you post so that people know who's work it is. It will not only keep people from using your work on their own websites but it will be instant advertising on any pics that are pinned or posted.

The awesome thing about these different forms of social media is they are free. They give people an idea of what your work is like. They can instantly go onto their phones and see if they are into the kind of hair you do.

If you don't have these sorts of accounts yet you might want to set them up. Another thing to remember is you want to use a moniker that is recognizable when it relates to your business. Try to avoid using things like plantlover77, it doesn't say anything about your hair business. Try something like styleyourhair82. Of course you can find one that sounds way cooler than that but you get the idea.

Social media is always a great way to post specials that your salon is running on product or services. Social media is an amazing forum for clients to interact with you and your salon as well. They can brag about your amazing talents online and start a conversation about hair tips and styling tricks.

There are so many creative ways to sell yourself. I know stylists who do fashions shows, wedding conventions, offer a free makeover to a silent auction or raffle, donate a product to a charity, and then talk about it on Facebook. It keeps you in the clients' mind and shows that you are active in your community. Post events that you've attended and hair shows that you are going to.

If you are watching new Youtube videos about haircutting then talk about it on your social media and get people interested in asking questions.

Some stylists even have blogs where they talk about hair tricks and tips. You would be surprised at the following of women that crave this kind of information. They are obsessed with learning how to use a round brush or the proper temperature for a curling iron.

You would be amazed at how many people just don't know the super simple stuff that we take for granted everyday like how to trim your bangs at home (because Lord knows every woman does it). They don't know what products to use for what hair type or how to care for their new color. How do you care for curly hair? There are a million things you can talk about on social media to give you street cred and visibility.

Dyeing to Get Repeat Clients

Now, let's talk client retention. Once you got 'em baited - hook, line, and sinker, what's next?

This is the best time to get your clients addicted to you and your hair magic! I love to help clients see that they made the best decision of their life by choosing to sit in my chair. I offer them beverages and I always give a lengthy head massage.

But before all of that happens, what about the consultation?

Consultations are so important with a new client and even clients that you've seen over 50 times for the last hundred years.

Clients have a choice to spend their money anywhere they want and they choose to spend it with you. If you forget to check in with a client when they sit down in your chair and make sure you are still meeting their needs then some other stylist out there will.

I love to greet my clients and then ask them one detailed question about something that has happened in their life. Usually this question has to do with something we've discussed on a previous appointment which makes clients feel special, like you are paying attention. If they are a new client then I will ask them about how they found me, or our salon, and thank them for being there.

With familiar clients I might say something like, "How was

your last haircut. Was is short enough?" They will usually respond with a few recommendations and then I will start their service.

With a new client the process goes very differently.

After I've thanked them for being there I may give them a quick tour of our salon. If I'm running more tightly on time I like to invite them to spend about 2 minutes talking about their expectations for the service. I will word it in a way that sounds polite but if you don't take the reigns here they are going to give you a short synapses of the past 15 years of bad haircuts. Your consult just turned into a 40 minute waste of time.

Be precise with your questions and take control. You are the one that wants to direct the conversation here. A simple way to sum up a consult is to let them know that you understand their needs by reflecting back to them key terms. This is so they know they are being heard.

These are some terms that seem to be a running theme in consultations:

- more volume
- more layers
- brighter highlights
- easier styling
- wash and go styling
- faster blow dry time
- face shape
- skin tone
- wanting more length
- bad last haircut

- brassiness/overly warm tones
- fading
- last stylist didn't listen
- something differently
- wants a change
- advice on product
- opinion on styles
- colors for the season

Once you get a good idea of key words, you can start to communicate in a way that the client understands.

Remember this very important key point: Clients are not stylists! They don't care about angles, tones, levels, or technical jargon. They want a certain feeling and a certain look, that's it.

I hear stylists every day who do the longest drawn-out consults on the planet which by the end of the client and the stylist are more confused than when they started. It's exhausting to listen to and frankly most clients know what their hair will and won't do. So when they come in with off the wall expectations just be honest. Were not necessary here to reinvent the color wheel.

Most clients will appreciate your honesty and they will not have false expectations that will only turn out to be a disappointment later on.

There was a lovely client that came to our salon when I first started doing hair. This client was one of the neediest and high maintenance clients I'd ever seen. She would come prancing in with a slew of the latest pictures she saw in US weekly and spent 20-45 minutes explaining how she wanted her hair to look. I didn't realize I could take control of the situation being fresh out of beauty school and this lady ran all over me.

At the end of the day her hair would never look like that picture, period! Putting up with this behavior takes a saint and I truly wanted to make this client happy but this is clearly not about hair. This is about her needy personality and her overbearing desire to feel special.

I've now learned in these cases that it is wise to be precise and stern. People need guidance and when they steer the ship it ends up like the Titanic. You are the professional. You do this job day in and day out. It's up to you to take the initiative and make it clear what is and what is not possible.

People know when they are being needy, draining, and demanding. Sometimes it takes a confident stylist to gently pull them back to reality. Tact is of utmost importance. Allow for some breathing room and patience in this process. I have found that I want the consultation to be smooth, short, and to the point.

After you have finished your service and you are completing their visit to the salon, remember to recommend at least three products they can purchase and then the most important part is next...

For the love of everything...GET THEM TO PRE-BOOK THEIR NEXT SERVICE!

I cannot tell you the thousands of times I've watched a stylist walk their client up to the front desk, drop them off, and run away. It takes two seconds to make sure they book their next service.

If you've ever been to a dentist office then you know that they make sure you are scheduled for your next 6 month cleaning without exception. Why are we any different? People need our skills and services and they need *you* to do it!

This small and simple step is vital and I mean vital with a capital "V." This ensures the future of a thriving business. Repeat clientele is the holy grail of hairstyling. Form this habit from the time you are a baby stylist and you will watch your business grow into a thriving giant.

If they give you an excuse like, "I don't know my schedule," or "I don't usually pre-book," PLAY DUMB!

Acknowledge their deflection and then rebuttal with, "You can always call or reschedule this appointment but it ensures you have a prime space in my busy schedule." Guests will usually book their appointment at that point and then you are guaranteed to have a flourishing schedule with lots of dollar signs all over it!

Another great way to keep the momentum going is to give your new clients a courtesy call after their first visit and make sure they are loving their new cut and color.

Our salon also does a survey for new clients through a computer program which keeps their contact info, alerts them about promotions, and sends them texts and emails to confirm appointments.

Clients love to feel needed and keeping in touch with them even electronically is a great way to make them feel like they are part of something that is growing and thriving. It's a nice little reminder that they matter and that without them you would not be succeeding.

There are other ways you can grow your business as well.

Referral programs are a great way to utilize the business that you already have, who already love you, and will spread the word for you.

Asking a few clients about what kind of incentives sound appealing to them is a great way to do some market research. In other words, what kind of goodies will make your clients want to tell the world about your amazing skills and talents as a stylist?

Here are a few ideas that could stir up some incentives:

- product discounts
- free conditioning treatment
- a free service with the referral of 3 new clients
- a dollar amount off for every referral
- gift cards
- entry into a drawing
- punch cards
- loyalty vouchers
- discounts for the referrer and referee

Get creative with your referral programs. Word of mouth is always going to be your best advertisement.

When I get a new referral it's very exciting because the client is already sold on my abilities. They are there because they've heard good things about me. They may still be a little scared and apprehensive but for the most part they are happy and excited to be there.

I love getting referred to a business. Usually the people I ask for recommendations from know me well enough to know if I'm going to click with whomever they are sending me to. I like the feeling of confidence and trust that comes with referrals.

If people are sending you referrals then make sure and acknowledge that. They will feel appreciated and it will encourage them to tell more people.

Customer service is huge when growing your new or old business. At our salon, we swoon over our clients like they just invented fire. It's always good to make sure that people feel welcomed.

Greeting clients the second they enter the door will immediately make them feel at ease. I've been to other businesses where I will walk in the door and stand there for a few minutes with no one saying anything to me. It's really frustrating and uncomfortable!

Make sure you greet your guests with a smile and let them know that they know you are happy they came to *your* salon as opposed to the salon down the street. I mentioned earlier that I may also take my new guests on a short tour of the salon. It really makes people feel like you are going the extra mile for them.

Show them where the restrooms are just in case they need them. Give them a brief run down of your retail area. Show them where tea and coffee are located if your salon offers beverages. If your salon has other services like nail or skin care then make sure and mention that too. Everyone loves convenience and if they can do everything in one spot, they are most likely going to get addicted to everyone in the salon and that can guarantee a more loyal client for you.

Once you've shown them around you can offer them a color smock if you're salon has those available so you don't ruin their

$400 purple label Ralph Lauren sweater (yes, I did that once). Then show them over to your work area. Make sure they know where to put all their accessories like their cell phone, purse, and sunglasses. Make them feel at home.

This time is their time away from life and they deserve to be pampered. You may be the only time that month that they are forced to sit still and have someone actually take care of *their* needs.

If I'm shampooing my own clients, I make sure that they are comfortable before starting the service. This next thing is big for me and I think it can make or break a great experience. I give every client a head massage with their shampoo. Yes it takes extra time, and yes it's not always convenient. But look at it this way...if you're not getting the job done then another stylist will!

A scalp massage is very relaxing for the client and also for the stylist. It gives you a chance to connect with them and relax their energy. It reminds them that they are doing something special for themselves.

If you have an assistant please make sure they know how to do a 3-5 minute massage with different manipulations. I learned this skill from the first stylist I assisted with and it has been my calling card ever since. My clients love my head massages. They are constantly making comments on how great it feels to have someone take that few extra minutes to make their visit extra special.

There are also specific health benefits to giving a scalp like lymphatic drainage and pressure points that can relieve stress. Take some time to learn some more specific details about the anatomy of the scalp. I find it very interesting to know that there are more than just feel good advantages to a good head massage.

Also, remember to keep conversations about yourself to a minimum and try to steer the conversation back to things that interest your client. Get to know their likes and dislikes. I've even seen stylists that will keep notes on a card or in the computer about client details. Things like: do they have kids, when did they take their last trip, what are their favorite foods, or what they do for work. If this helps you to keep track then by all means take notes.

Clients are the reason we show up to work in the morning and they are the reason we are able to live the life we want. Make their visit super special and I guarantee they will make you feel special by supporting your business.

Growing your business happens when you care about it. Treat it like your baby and your most valuable asset. It's priceless and when you put energy into it, it will come back to you tenfold. You will reap the fruit of all your hard work. It's a guaranteed investment and the key to your success.

Dyeing to Sell Products

I can already hear you getting uncomfortable. Almost every stylist I know hates selling.

There is a huge reason why most stylists are not selling product and that is because they are thinking within their own pocket book. The number one rule of selling product is to assume that your guest has millions to spend.

I know it's hard to grasp this concept because we might be thinking, "Mary already spent like 150 dollars on her hair, she's not going to want to buy 100 dollars in product too!," right? WRONG!

This could be the furthest thing in the world from the truth. The key here is knowing your products and then helping Mary to realize that she needs the product to make her hair look the way you did.

Statistics show that clients are more likely to buy hair products right after a hair service than any other time. It's already on their mind. The pipes are primed and ready to go. If you don't sell them the right shampoo and conditioner to maintain their color they will most likely drive down to the next beauty supply in the nearest mall and buy the products from them.

If they go somewhere else for product the likelihood that they will buy the product that you would want them using is very low.

Think of this, most of the people working at beauty supplies in the mall don't have a license to do hair - you do!

I've taken lots of product knowledge classes and most of the product educators will tell you the same thing: Recommend at least 3 products that your guest could potentially use and they will buy at least one if not all three.

Even if someone insists that they don't need anything, just offer friendly knowledge about the products that you're using in their hair and explain all the amazing benefits that it will give them. It doesn't even have to sound like a sales pitch. It can sound like you're having a conversations with a friend. If your salon is generous enough to offer samples and they seem intrigued, make sure they walk out of your salon with one.

For example, I love this one product that our salon carries and it's absolutely a must have! I use it on every single client, man or woman, short or long hair. This one product is a heat protectant, UV protectant, and detangler in one. I mean, who wouldn't want that at home right!?

I might sell it to a guest like this:

> "This product that I'm spraying into your hair is 3 products in one. It will protect your hair from the heat of blow drying and curling. It will help protect your color from fading in the sun, and it helps detangle knots. Plus it smells like the beach. I use this product on every single client and it's never a good idea to go out the door with naked hair."

We both get a good laugh and if they want to know more they will ask me a few question. If they're not interested then we go on to how their kids are doing or gab about their work. Whatever the outcome, I shared some pretty valuable knowledge with them and they get to decide if that product is something they want to invest in.

Products are so important to the maintenance of your work. If you just bought a new Ferrari wouldn't you want to know how to take care of the paint and interior. You wouldn't just throw dish soap on a scrubber and start washing the outside of it. You would want the right tools and that is what professional hair products are all about.

An advantage to being a stylist and working with hair everyday is we know that hair needs certain products to stay healthy and get desired results. We can use this knowledge to help the guest realize that they have a need for what we are selling.

Creating a need is vital in product selling.

If their hair feels dry, there's a need for moisture. If their hair is curly and they want to dry it straight then they have a need for a thermal straightener. Most clients, even the low maintenance ones, use shampoo if nothing else. Make sure they are using something professional in their shower at home.

Identify a need in their hair regime and help the guest come up with a product solution that will fit their need.

Specific product knowledge is so vital when it comes to selling product.

I know the last thing most stylists want to do is take time out of their busy schedule to educate themselves on product. It seems boring and daunting, especially because we like to create. But knowing our products will give us confidence. Specific details will make the product we are selling more appealing.

If you walked into a fancy department store and started asking about their shoes I guarantee that sales person will know all sorts of things about those shoes that you didn't expect. Things like what materials they use, the kind of support they offer, the dyes used, etc. This detailed information makes these shoes suddenly seem more valuable, interesting, and unique.

The reason stores keep their employees trained is because anytime you are selling the little facts and details make your product seem way more intriguing and the product instantly seems more valuable.

If you know nothing about the products at your salon besides the fact that one is for volume and one is for color-treated hair then you aren't going to sell very many products. You're probably going to look like you're fumbling when a client wants to know if there are sulfates in that shampoo or not. The more you sound like you know what you are talking about when selling product, the more your client will get excited about wanting to buy them. Products will deliver the results they're looking for at home.

Trends are always changing in the realm of hair products. One year it's all about keratin and the next year it's all about sulfates. It's so beneficial to keep up on these trends so clients stay educated when they hear about the latest shampoo or conditioner.

Don't be that stylist who hears about that new ground breaking product for the first time from your client who just read about in Vogue magazine.

If you are not able to take a class because of schedule restraints then talk with your local rep about the product details. Most reps will be more than happy to spend time with you because when you're selling, they're making commissions.

It will do you a world of good to stay up on the latest products your salon is carrying. Remember these key points when selling products:

- create a need
- know your products
- keep the conversation light
- recommend at least 3 products
- assume guests have millions to spend

Selling may be your least favorite thing to do in the salon but it's an integral part of your success. Don't miss out on this untapped source of income for you and your salon. Selling your clients the products they need will keep their hair looking beautiful and every time they use those products at home they will think about their amazing stylist.

Dyeing to Set Healthy Boundaries

A career as a stylist is a marathon and not a race. There are a few important things to remember when dealing with the public that will ensure you have a long and fulfilling life as a stylist.

The first thing to remember is to set healthy boundaries with clients. This can spill out into many different areas, even time spent with clients outside of the salon.

My time is very valuable and I've found that over the years I have had to become very realistic about how much my body can handle and how much energy I have to give at work. If I know that I can work 8 hours a day and that's it then I have to honor that time by sticking to a schedule.

So many times I see stylists trying to squeeze people in here and there; coming in early and staying extra late. I am hereby granting every stylist the power to say "no!" It's not natural for us to say no for two reasons. 1) We like making money and 2) Most of us are people-pleasers.

I have had to learn to stick to my guns when scheduling clients. If I don't I will burn out. I will end up stretching myself so thin that there won't be anything left to give. I have learned the value of self-management and self-preservation.

I remember the days when I was stacking clients like pancakes and trying to get everyone and their sister in for a last minute color. It took its toll on my mind and body. I not only started wearing down and suffering from stress but I started to resent my clients. If you over do it your body will eventually tell you that it's done being pushed to the limits. Don't get to the point that I did where I was lying in a hospital bed literally stressing the life out of myself. Life is more than your job and your clients.

If someone is begging to get in with you and you have absolutely no place to get them in then it isn't your fault that they didn't plan ahead. Offer them the option of seeing another stylist at the salon who is building and spread the love around. It will come back to you in the form of relief and it will help everyone at the salon to stay busy. I like to see everyone at our salon succeeding and thriving. If I can refer a client out to someone I trust that we all win and the salon doesn't lose any business.

When a guest chooses to see another stylist in the salon I always try to make an effort to go over and let them know that their presence is appreciated and that I am happy to see them. We're all adults here and there should only be room for the success of the whole. If someone is not playing nice in the sandbox and resentment builds because a client decided they liked another stylist better then remember that is not your issue. Put your big girl pants on, build a bridge, and get over it sister!

I get excited when everyone is busy and in the flow. Imagine, the salon is buzzing and the success starts to become contagious. I truly believe the success of the salon I work at is contributed to this principle. Our owners don't have an egotistic bone in their bodies and when we succeed, they succeed. It's creates a beautiful synergy of abundance.

Many times clients feel like we are their best friend and while we are good at building relationships with our guests we also want to make sure that we are continuing to uphold an attitude of professionalism. Going out and getting smashed with a client on the weekends is probably not the best way to build a business.

I had a situation when I was first starting to do hair that cured me of the silly notion that I needed to be best buds with my clients.

I was invited to go out with a client for drinks but when I showed up, Miss Peggy Sue (names have been changed to protect the innocent) was already 3 and a half sheets to the wind. The second I walked up to say hello, she tried to french kiss me in front of my partner and the rest of creation. I was so completely mortified that I jerked back in disbelief. Sadly I lost that client right there and then.

So with that lesson learned I now choose to be extremely scrutinizing with what clients I spend time with outside of the salon. God forbid I ever have to go through that again.

Following a guideline of ethics with clients is a wise and prudent idea in business and I want to name a few ideas here that you might want to put into practice.

- Decline awkward private social invitations politely.
- Avoid giving out your home address.
- Keep texting conversations limited to business.
- Always schedule appointments during business hours.
- Stick to your schedule times.
- Charge a full or fair price, even to friends.

There will be times of course where these rules can be bent. Just always remember to respect yourself as numero uno. If it doesn't feel right, don't do it.

As I finish this book up, I want to encourage and remind you that you don't have to sacrifice yourself to make money. I know stylists who are literally killing themselves behind the chair. I used to be one of them. Nothing is worth your health, sanity, joy, and peace of mind. There will always be plenty of business in the world to go around and when the time comes to give yourself a raise don't be afraid of losing business. Raising your prices is a necessary and vital part of being a stylist. We work hard and deserve to be compensated.

Opposed to contrary belief we *do* work hard. I love how clients are always saying how fun our jobs must be and yes, that is true, but it is also very physically and emotionally demanding. Staying centered and balanced is the name of the game.

Have fun and remember to play! If you love your job, your salon, and your fellow stylists, then you are setting yourself up for major success. Once you've honed your skills, the business and the clients will automatically start to find their way into your chair.

Like a moth to a flame, no one can resist a well-rounded hair stylist. We style the world and lead the fashion industry with our talent and vision. You are the forerunner of beauty as the world sees it and your unique style is what fuels the world of trends.

Stay true to your extraordinary authenticity and bring your talent to the masses. In the end it's about doing what you love and loving what you do. We get to color the world beautiful and what a wonderful way to earn a living when you dye to make hairy money.

www.ingramcontent.com/pod-product-compliance
Lightning Source LLC
Chambersburg PA
CBHW070919180526
45168CB00005B/2075

9 781512 380231